THE
COLLABORATIVE
Artist

T0087333

Bettyian Roulade

by NANCY FABER

FOR C FLUTE

Commissioned by Dr. Penelope Peterson Fischer
in appreciation of her teacher Betty Bang Mather

World Premiere, National Flute Convention
Las Vegas, Nevada • August 10, 2012

FABER
PIANO ADVENTURES®

ISBN 978-1-61677-708-1

Key to Performance Terms

T-CHR	"Tea-cher." Loud tongued syllables for a percussive effect
x	Key slap with L.H. finger 3
	square-note shape Finger the natural note and overblow a higher harmonic.
n.v.	non vibrato
add v.	add vibrato
↑	roll out (sharp)
↓	roll in (flat)
→	normal pitch
	Finger the diamond-shaped lower note. Overblow to achieve the harmonic pitch of the upper note.
,	breath mark and slight pause
F.T.	flutter tongue
(trill key 2)	Example flute fingering diagram ● indicates key depressed ∅ indicates tremolo

Bettyian Roulade

Flute

Nancy Faber
(b. 1955)

Flute

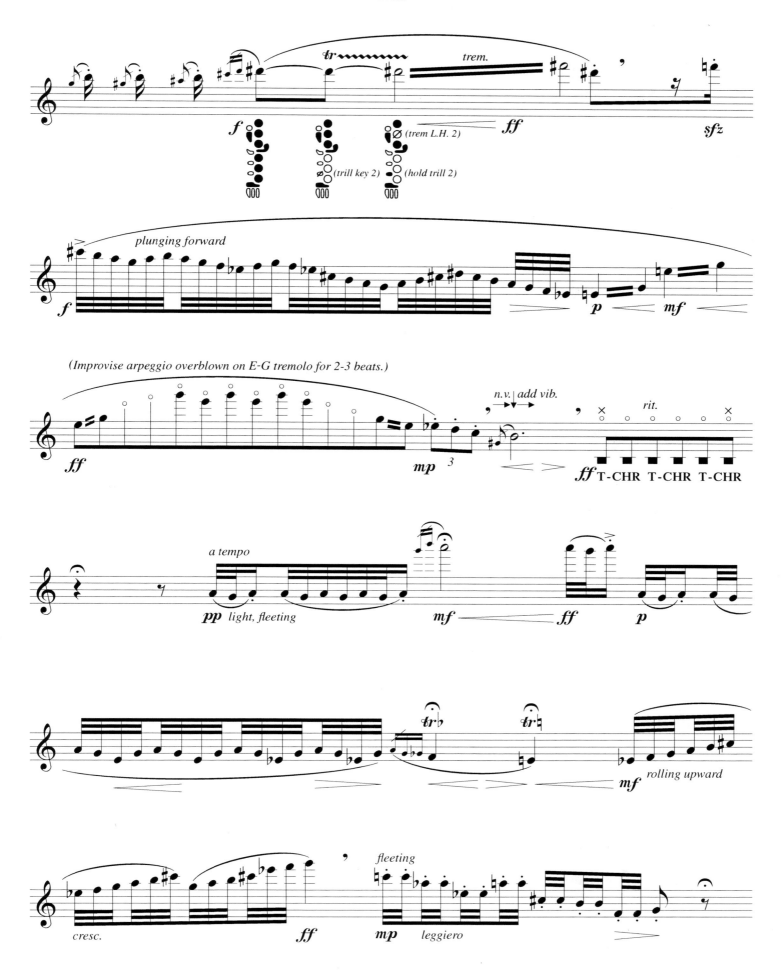

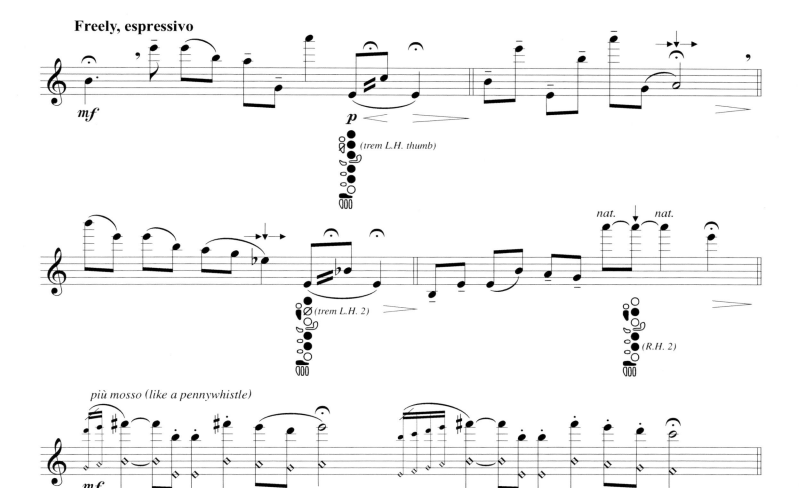

Flute

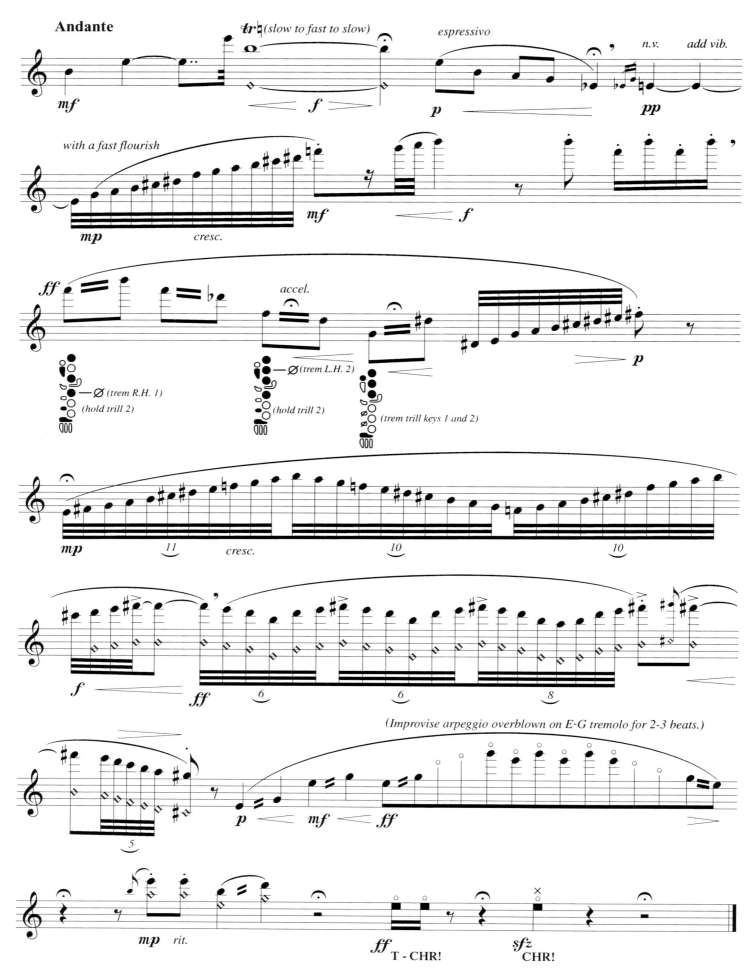